The Ripple Effect

Written By

Strategic Coach® Clients

for Dan Sullivan

ISBN-10: 1499528906
ISBN-13: 978-1499528909

Here's What's Inside

6   Foreword by Dean Jackson and Joe Polish

9   Introduction by Michael Williams

12   "Dan Sullivan brought me into the arena of the 21st century" by Greg Powell

15   "Dan taught me how to transition from a personality-driven business to a process-driven business" by Tim Goodwin

18   "Dan has taught us the difference between intellectual property and intellectual capital" by Gary Boomer

21   "Walking into a room of Strategic Coach peers is like walking into a brotherhood" by Robert Saik

25   "What's the one thing that would motivate you and excite you for the rest of your life?" by Dean Jackson

27   "Dan was instrumental in my transformation from financial services product pusher to value creator" by Mark Westcott

30   "Dan takes a much bigger approach to goal setting, which paints the picture of where you want to be in 20 years" by Sally Colocho

34   "Dan made my impossible dream very ordinarily achievable" by Steven Palter, M.D.

38 "Dan is an applied philosopher who helps you improve your world using the power of your mind" by Michele Palter

40 "You can have all the success in the world, but if you don't have gratitude, you're not going to be happy" by Joe Polish

45 "Envision who you have to be in the future when your business is ten times larger" by Joseph Cohen

47 "You know you've found your Unique Ability when you can do it all day long, and, at the end of the day, you're not tired in the least" by Steven Jackson

49 "Perfection, not progress, is what holds a lot of entrepreneurs back" by Peter Kaplan

50 "Dan showed me how to work smarter in my business, but more than anything how to work on my business and have a personal life as well" by Patrick Keating

54 "Dan showed me it's not about me being significant but what significant impact I was going to have on the world" by Roch Tranel

57 "With Dan's help, we've increased our asset base by over 800% and we've taken our equity 10x" by Braden Hodye

60 "Dan's Lifetime Extender exercise has shifted my thinking so that rather than thinking about retiring and hanging it up, I have a vision of another 50 years of contribution" by Mrya Salzer

63 "Dan showed me that you get paid a lot more when you offer a transformation than you do when you offer a transaction" by Ken Losch

66 "Thanks to Dan, we're transforming the industry and having a lot of fun doing it" by Bob Muller

69 "Frank Sinatra didn't move pianos" by Joseph Johnson

71 "Dan showed me that thinking 10x is far better than thinking 2x, because with 2x you're not really working toward becoming a different you" by Ninad Tipnis

74 "Time isn't a scarce resource. It's actually an abundance resource if you use it right" by Bob Mulhern

77 "For me, Coach is my insurance policy moving forward" by Christopher Phelps

80 "I have learned how to think differently about growth and multiplying different results" by Michael Williams

83 Biography of Dan Sullivan

Foreword

What can we say about our good friend Dan Sullivan? It's amazing to stop and think about how impactful one man can be. Dan's going to be seventy this year—an age when most people are looking to retire and hang it up. Not Dan. He's looking 25 years out to creating an even bigger future for himself and those around him. He has no intention of slowing down, and so the ripple he is making will continue to expand and expand.

Dan Sullivan has been coaching and changing lives for over 40 years now. Little did we know when we met Dan back in the late '90s how much of an impact he would have, not only on our own lives but in our businesses and our thinking. Stop and think about how many people have better lives and bigger futures as a result of knowing Dan. Dan coaches his clients to play a much bigger game on a much larger scale, and, as a result, he improves the lives of thousands of people he's never even met. That's an inspiring and uplifting thought.

One of Dan's Unique Abilities is working with and improving the lives of people who have the ability to make real waves in the world. Dan focuses his efforts on entrepreneurs who want to make positive change and leave a significant impact. By choosing to work with achievement-minded entrepreneurs, Dan's reach is not only greater, he models for us what he teaches, which is how to make the best use of our time on this planet.

We only get so many years to make our mark. Why not reach the largest number of people you can? Why not reach for 10x growth? Don't settle for 2x growth when you can change and evolve your thinking to reach 10x more people than you're reaching now. If you can reach and touch hundreds of people and make their lives better, how much better will the planet be if you can instead reach thousands if not hundreds of thousands? That's the power of hanging around a guy like Dan. He stretches you and challenges you to be an Industry Transformer™, to reach more people by bettering yourself and expanding your reach.

Dan seeks out entrepreneurs who are making a difference and helps them become 5% better, 10% better, and in some cases, double, triple, quadruple, and 10x their productivity and profitability, which in turn quadruples the impact and influence they have on their clients, customers, patients, and the world.

From knowing Dan and being in his Program, we've learned how to be better listeners, how to get better at focusing in this busy world, and, most of all, how to be better entrepreneurs and human beings.

The full effect Dan has made by helping those who can really impact the world is beyond what we can conceive. We are truly excited to be a part of this book and to read the stories of how Dan has had a ripple effect in the lives of his clients. It's amazing to think this all started for me so many years ago with a simple Knowledge Product Dan wrote that I found— and look where the journey has taken me all these years later. Dan was able to take an idea and package it in a way that had an impact on me even before I met him. That's an inspiring concept when you follow it through. Dan reaches people he will never even meet.

We're excited to introduce you to the impact one man has had on the landscape. We invite you into the world of entrepreneurs from all of over the world who are doing what they can to make an impact. We hope that, one day, you too are part of the ripple Dan started 40 years ago.

Dean & Joe

Introduction

May 2014
Toronto, Canada

For over 20 years, the Strategic Coach® Program has empowered more than 16,000 entrepreneurs to transform their businesses and enhance their quality of life. Many entrepreneurs have applied what they learn at Strategic Coach® and have exponentially grown their profitability, impact, and—my personal favorite—their free time!

Strategic Coach was founded and is currently led by an incredible man, Dan Sullivan. Dan is turning 70 years old this May. As a coach client, I wondered how we could honor a man who has had such a profound impact on so many lives. The idea of writing this book came to me when I was working on a Strategic Coach tool at my quarterly workshop in Chicago last January. This book is dedicated to Dan on his 70th Birthday so he is able to hear a small sample of the impact he has had in the lives of his clients. In essence, we desire for him to see the true "Ripple Effect" he has had in this world. You will hear stories of Strategic Coach clients who have multiplied their business and grown in an exponential way. As a result, they are able to reach and change the lives of more people and the cycle continues.

Not only did we want to show our appreciation to Dan, we wanted to give him a gift that Strategic Coach could use to exponentially grow the number of clients in the program. This book is 100% client-driven and client-organized. We hope you, the reader, will be inspired, motivated, and encouraged to join the journey of reaching new heights in your life by joining Strategic Coach with us. This is an invitation for you to join the community of exponential thinkers who are making a tremendous impact and difference in the lives of many people throughout the world through their business.

This compilation of stories of impact from current coach clients around the world is a surprise to Dan. We could only hope to have even the slightest ripple effect that Dan has had. Why not be a part of it? Jump in and let the ripples roll.

To Your Success!

Michael Williams

"I alone cannot change the world, but I can cast a stone across the waters to create many ripples."

—Mother Teresa

*"**D**an Sullivan brought me into the arena of the 21st century."*

Greg Powell
-FI Plan Partners

How do I thank somebody who has transformed my life like Dan Sullivan has transformed mine? How do I express my appreciation for all he has done? Not only for me personally, but also professionally? The effect he's had, not only in terms of my family, but in terms of my entire business and organization, the people I work with, the clients I have, almost can't be quantified.

I can vividly remember hearing about Dan Sullivan from various colleagues when I got a copy of his *21st Century Agent*. Keep in mind the *21st Century Agent* book was written in 1995. In 1995, Dan Sullivan was already projecting out what the 21st century was going to look like in terms of the financial services industry.

I read that book cover to cover all in one day and was just blown away by the insight Dan shared. As a professional in the financial services industry who was looking to be on the cutting edge, to be a leader in my field and in what I was doing, not only in how to make money and increase net worth for our clients, but also on how to be a visionary myself in terms of understanding where the industry is headed, there was no better place for me to learn.

In the financial services industry, we talk about forecasting economics and trends, and what the economy's going to look like as we go forward, but we're all guilty of not taking the time and doing it in our own business. Dan Sullivan showed me that I needed to take charge of my practice in a whole different way.

There are times when Dan is sharing his ideas with us where you want to stand up and shout, "Do you realize what you've just done for my life? Do you realize how much money I can generate in revenue for my organization as a result if this one idea? Do you realize the relationships you've just transformed for me with the people I work with?"

Now here I am in the 21st century, and my business is thriving like never before. My personal life and my family are doing fantastic. The way I've learned to balance my personal life with my career and my business has been huge for me, all because of the ideas and vision of this one man named Dan Sullivan.

It was Teddy Roosevelt who said:

"It is not the critic who counts; not the man who points out how the strong man stumbles, or where the doer of deeds could have done them better. The credit belongs to the man who is actually in the arena, whose face is marred by dust and sweat and blood, who strives valiantly; who errs and comes short again and again; because there is not effort without error and shortcomings; but who does actually strive to do the deed; who knows the great enthusiasm, the great devotion, who spends himself in a worthy cause, who at the best knows in the end the triumph of high achievement and who at the worst, if he fails, at least he fails while daring greatly. So that his place shall never be with those cold and timid souls who know neither victory nor defeat."

My response today to Dan Sullivan is thank you, because you have brought me into the arena of the 21st century. Because of you, I fully understand victory, how to plan for victory, that I have a "Moving Future" I can control, and how to make a difference in my life and in all the lives around me.

No one is successful unless they touch the lives around them, and they'll never be fulfilled unless they're making a difference. Because of you, Dan, I don't understand failure; because of you, failure is not an option. I have the opportunity to tap into an environment to constantly create, to reinvent, to innovate, to come up with new ideas, and to be cutting edge. Because of Strategic Coach, I cannot only change my life, but the lives of everybody around me.

To you, Dan Sullivan, I say thank you from the bottom of my heart. Thank you for what you've done for me. I hope you have an incredibly happy 70th birthday. I'm looking forward to being in your class, learning from you when you're ninety-five and one hundred and five. God bless you, Dan Sullivan, for all you've done.

*"**D**an taught me how to transition from a personality-driven business to a process-driven business."*

Tim Goodwin
-Goodwin Investments

When I joined Strategic Coach, I was doing everything by myself in my business, I was working more hours than I wanted to, and I was stressed out all the time because of it. I knew I had no time to come up with new ideas for growing my business, as I was always putting out fires and chasing new business.

One of the biggest takeaways for me from working with Dan has been empowering me to hire the right people and fire the ones who aren't a fit. But, bigger than that, Dan got me to make this really big transition from having a personality-driven business to having a process-driven business.

When I say personality-driven business, I mean that the clients are hiring you for you, not because of your company. They do business with you because of their relationship with you. Maybe it's because they're friends with you. They already trust you because you have this pre-existing relationship.

We did a customer/client satisfaction survey and asked our clients, "What do you like the most about our company?" or "What do you like the most about our service?" or "What really stands out to you?" and the answers kept coming back, "Tim is great. We like Tim. We trust Tim."

For some people, answers like those would make them feel really good, but it didn't make me feel good. In fact, it kind of made me feel bad. Here I was really trying to build a business with a team and yet all they could see was my personality and how much they liked me.

Shortly after I joined Coach, we started developing our company's Unique Processes™, putting names to those processes, and introducing those to our clients. We started addressing ourselves as a team and how we provide the professional service, as a team to them. I wanted customers and clients coming to our firm, not because of me, the personality, but because of the company and the process and the uniqueness of the processes and tools and services we offer our clients.

As a result of this shift, just three and a half years after being in Coach, I have doubled my income, and my company went from just me to a team of six.

Now, because I have a business that doesn't depend solely on me, I can step away from the business and know things won't fall apart and that the clients are being serviced well. The processes are in place. Because of this, I now spend a lot more time at home with my family.

I wanted to take this opportunity to thank Dan Sullivan for creating this company so long ago, for being an unique individual who would skip class in grade school to go to the library and read and think and to compile all the wisdom he has and to create a program that has not just been a blessing to me, but to my family and clients.

Coach has been a blessing to my team as they get to have jobs they love to come to and get a lot of satisfaction out of.

My clients have been impacted as well as they appreciate having clear value articulated and clear systems, processes, and tools in place to help them reach their goals.

I wanted to thank you, Dan, and I hope this is an encouragement for others to join Coach. I will be forever indebted.

*"**D**an has taught us the difference between intellectual property and intellectual capital."*

Gary Boomer
-Boomer Consultants Inc.

Dan Sullivan is truly a Multiplier Leader and coach. He leverages your Unique Abilities and provides you with the tools to think, plan, and grow. He has taught us the difference between intellectual property and intellectual capital, plus the power of using graphics. In fact, after almost 20 years in the Program, we have trademarked the phrase Think, Plan, Grow™.

Dan has shown us that intellectual property is something you protect and only use yourself. Intellectual capital is something you share so your entire client base benefits. While we have the trademark to Think, Plan, Grow™, our clients benefit from the concept.

Dan has had an extremely positive impact on me as an entrepreneur, on my family, on my business associates, and on my clients. We have leveraged Dan's knowledge, teaching, and tools in our consulting practice to provide tremendous value to our clients. Dan talks about how all value is created by Leadership (direction), Relationship (confidence), and Creativity (capability). This has proven true in our markets, which are larger accounting firms and closely held businesses.

It has been interesting to experience Dan's thinking and confidence grow as he has now coached some of the most successful entrepreneurs in many industries—true Industry Transformers. While they have provided real-life experiences, Dan has provided them with a safe environment to think and the tools to solve many of the problems associated with running a business. His most recent breakthrough of 10x thinking was several years in advance of Jim Collins who researched and wrote *Great by Choice*, but primarily focused on public companies. Dan's thinking and strategies are based on entrepreneurs and small business and the importance of thinking 10x rather than incrementally. He has also stressed 10x thinking is not just about revenue, but all facets of the company, including service, processes, and profits.

Dan's guidance and coaching have provided me with great confidence and insight about the changes needed in the accounting profession. Many of these changes are driven by technology, an area of expertise that our company has focused on. Dan has helped our company address the issues and focus on the necessary changes rather than the results as most accountants tend to do. A quote from Jack Dixon emphasizes the point: "If you focus on results, you will never change. If you focus on change, you will get results." Dan's tools such as the Impact Filter™ and The Strategy Circle® are used daily in our firm.

Dan has also taught me that with entrepreneurship and innovation comes failure. Not every idea works, and most great ideas are resisted by most of your peers due to the fact that ideas require change. Great examples of this in our profession are hourly pricing and advisory services. Most accountants are still wanting to provide compliance-based services (tax and accounting) while clients are looking for advisory services based upon improved performance of their business and strategic plans focused on growth or succession. Clients also want fixed prices rather than hourly. Dan has made me a better consultant and leader in our market. For that, I am extremely grateful.

Most importantly, Dan, at age seventy, has committed to another 25 years. He has the passion, health, and innovative ideas to keep himself and other leading entrepreneurs engaged at an age when most people are looking at retirement and entitlements. He is truly future-focused. Entrepreneurs are wired differently than most, and Dan understands their needs and the needs of their Unique Ability® Teams. Thank you, Dan, for all you do for us.

*"**W**alking into a room of Strategic Coach peers is like walking into a brotherhood."*

Robert Saik
-Agri-Trend®

I'm a perfect candidate for Strategic Coach because I'm a slow learner and it's taken me almost 20 years of working with Dan Sullivan to figure out that a Free Day™ isn't a day you work all day for free—it's actually meant for rejuvenation.

In 1994, I was contemplating leaving the corporate world and becoming an entrepreneur. I enrolled in Strategic Coach and it was really the catalyst for me to start my own organization, which I began in 1997 called Agri-Trend®. Agri-Trend consists of agri-coaches, market coaches, business coaches, and geo-coaches who provide services to farmers using strategic processes, such as The Strategic Crop Plan, The Strategic Marketing Plan, and The Strategic Farm Business Plan.

They say imitation is the sincerest form of flattery. If that's true, I can honestly tell you Agri-Trend is a Strategic Coach company, and we have integrated many of the components from Strategic Coach into the very soul of Agri-Trend. Everything from the Impact Filter and Strategy Circle to the 30-, 60-, 90-Day, and One-Year Planners. Those tools and the strategic thinking that Dan has provided permeated our company, and we use them as a foundation onto which we've built our entire team and organization.

One of the most consistent things in my life has been Dan Sullivan and Strategic Coach. It doesn't matter what's going on professionally or personally—I know every 90 days I get to go in that room of like-minded individuals, I get a grounding to refocus my energies, and I get to look back at all the successes we are actually having rather than being overwhelmed by all the problems that exist on my plate today or the perceived failures we've had.

It seems that the more "successful" you become, the more isolated you become, because fewer and fewer people actually understand you. They don't understand what drives you. And I have to say walking into a room of Strategic Coach peers is like walking into a brotherhood because it doesn't matter what the industry is—if they're a plastic surgeon or a grocery owner supermarket owner in New York City or a lumber business down in North Carolina—you know they're dealing with the same problems and challenges you are. When we do our breakout sessions at Strategic Coach, it's really nice to be able to interface and talk with like minded-individuals.

One of the things we've done at Agri-Trend is to bring in some of Dan's team, like team expert Shannon Waller, to facilitate planning sessions inside of our business. Every year, we have something called a super summit, which is a gathering of all the Agri-Trend key personnel, and Strategic Coach has come into our business and facilitated these training sessions largely to create commonality of language and to harmonize many of the tools I use as an entrepreneur into our team and indeed right down to our farm customer level. What this does is start to give us a common framework of being able to speak to each other. For example, I won't do a meeting with my team unless the team has filled out an Impact Filter ahead of time, which is basically a clear understanding of why we're having the meeting and the success criteria and the ideal outcome of that meeting.

When my team does this, it is very energizing and, quite frankly, it also prevents a large waste of time. I know from my perspective, I use the Strategic Coach tools with my team on a daily basis. I use it with my executive assistant, I use it in my personal life with my family to share what we're going to do in the coming year or the coming quarter, and I use it to plan out my personal as well as my business time.

One of the other benefits of being in Coach has been the push Dan's given to me as an individual. He's pushed me to do things like write a book, he's challenged me to hire additional people to support me, and as I break through these Ceilings of Complexity that Dan will talk about, or as I break through these barriers, my life only gets richer and better. I live a wonderful big life, and I don't know if I would have had the same degree of progress had I not been with Dan and Strategic Coach.

Thank you, Dan! Here's to another 20 years with you at the helm as we grow and change.

*"**W**hat's the one thing that would motivate you and excite you for the rest of your life?"*

Dean Jackson
-New Information!

My first exposure that I had to Dan Sullivan was through the Knowledge Product, *How The Best Get Better*®. The first thing I was struck with was how professional everything looked. Everybody knows Dan has an incredible design eye and everything about the environment of Strategic Coach, whether it's being touched through info, through Knowledge Products, through the offices, which are incredible, the experience, the food—everything is first-class. That was something that really struck me.

I remember just being impacted by how different this was because you and I both came from a world of direct response where ugly was the way of the day. It was really ugly info products getting out there. I knew immediately this was something different.

When Dan started his new group, I think it was in 2009, I joined right away, and it's been an amazing reflection to look back that since the first time of being in the Program that I had 10x my income from when I first joined Strategic Coach in 1997. Dan was talking about and revolving everything around this notion of 10x your income. Initially, it sounds like a lot, and it sounds like a lot of work, but he counterbalances it with this idea of the Self-Managing Company. The combination of 10x growth but with self-managing has been the biggest impact on me. I'm in for as long the 25-year plan.

I think that most of the people who are impacted by Dan are getting into this idea of having a 25-year relationship. It's unique to hear a 70-year-old guy talking about his 25-year plan and surrounding himself with people who are thinking 25 years out and thinking 10x.

What Dan would call an "Abundance Neighborhood" has had an amazing impact on me, going through this conscious thought of what a 10x organization would look like in my own business. That's been an incredible thinking process. That idea of Thinking About Your Thinking underneath the umbrella of your big picture goal of 10x and balancing that with a Self-Managing Company—it's been amazing to be able to set up divisions of my own company, which are now completely self-managing, that were inspired by being in relationship with Dan and being in conversation with Dan and raising the level of the thinking I have about my business.

So many things I do were inspired by being around Dan—doing all the Breakthrough Blueprint Events came out of a conversation with Dan where he asked, "What's the one thing that would motivate you and excite you for the rest of your life?" That was the answer: spending time with people, applying marketing to their specific business, to a variety of businesses that's exciting to me. Being inspired by Dan to write books and to create a process called "The 90-Minute Book," to be able to offer that service to people. It's how we're doing this book right now. All of that is "The Ripple Effect" of having met and been introduced to Dan Sullivan through an information product back in 1996.

Dan, it's been an amazing journey, and I very much am looking forward to the next 25 years with you!

*"**D**an was instrumental in my transformation from financial services product pusher to value creator."*

Mark Westcott
-The Strategic Evolution™

Before I met Dan Sullivan, I was an absolute workaholic with no balance in my life. And, whilst doing well financially, I just didn't have the balance I needed and craved.

Dan's program provided the structured thinking that was missing for me. The 90-day time frame between getting together was just the right amount of time to affect my thinking and allow me to shape my strategy. It allowed me to get things implemented before the next meeting.

One of the greatest aspects of being part of Strategic Coach is the community of like-minded peers. It's turning up each quarter and sitting in a room with a bunch of entrepreneurs who are mostly way more successful than I am. It's given me the ability to tap into the different aspects and perspectives on life and business and to be able to learn from everyone in the room and to associate with people in the room, each of whom are powerfully successful in their own right.

One of the most powerful concepts Dan taught me was understanding the value creation process. I watched Dan talk about entrepreneurs who said they could get rid of their financial licenses and create a Unique Process™ for their clients and charge an upfront fee. This was very eye-opening for me. To get away from being the commodity salesman to creating a fee-based Unique Process is a huge shift. Two and a half years ago, I sold my financial planning practice and was able to get rid of my finance license once and for all. I became free from the bureaucratic and compliance nightmare that has gripped the industry.

What this also did for me was to move from selling products and looking after hundreds if not thousands of policy holders of life insurance and financial products, to utilizing a fee-based Unique Process that's based on value creation. Now we have relationships with about 40 or so high net worth clients who pay me upfront for solving their dangers and issues.

For that opportunity and peace of mind, they write me significant checks for the value I create. Because of that, I don't need to deal with as many people. I have much better balance in my life, and I'm able to choose the people I want to deal with. Another fabulous outcome of working with Dan is that now, every client is someone I want to deal with. They're people I like, people I like hanging out with, and they're friends, not just clients. That's been the change that Dan has made in my life, because I was able to give up the commodity world and turn into someone who creates unique value for a small number of people who are prepared to write a check for having that personal attention and value.

So many other people in the financial services industry are being drowned by bureaucratic structures, compliance, and regulation. It was such a liberating thing for me to be able to walk away from all that and be free to utilize my Unique Ability® and value-creation process for the clients I love.

Certainly, of all the concepts Dan has come up with, the concepts of Unique Ability and creating a Unique Process have changed my life. To me they are two of the key concepts of the whole Strategic Coach® Program.

Because of Dan's contribution to the world in general and his contribution to my own business and personal life, my life has evolved. It shows in the work I do with my clients. I'm able to pass on such great wisdom, knowledge, and capability to the people I deal with. For that, Dan, I take my hat off to you.

It's been a privilege to be with you in every workshop I've attended over the past 15 years. It's been a privilege to listen to your words of wisdom and your insights and to take those ideas and shape and change my life and the lives of all the people I'm involved with.

I'm not sure Dan will ever understand the magnitude of the multiplier effect he's on the world. His coaching leads us to take the message and ideas out into the community to help other people. The number of people positively impacted multiplies. Throughout the world, many people are now in a better place in their lives because of Dan Sullivan.

Dan, I salute you. Happy birthday from a land "Down Under."

*"**D**an takes a much bigger approach to goal setting, which paints the picture of where you want to be in 20 years. "*

Sally Colocho
- deciBel Research, Inc.

Strategic Coach had an impact on my life even before we actually joined the Program. I read something in a book once, and it pointed me to Strategic Coach. I went to one of Dan's half-day seminars with my husband for my birthday. During the seminar, Dan talked about Unique Ability and explained how everybody has something they're passionate about and they do well, and we should take the time to find out what that is and do that. The example he gave was that not everybody likes to drive, so why would you drive to work every day? Why not hire someone to drive you, if someone would love to do it? In fact—I'll never forget it—the example he gave was, "I'm sure there are plenty of unemployed Ph.Ds who'd love to drive. Why not employ one of them to drive you around?"

Within two weeks of Dan's talk, I bought myself a nice car and handed the keys to my husband, who happens to be a Ph.D in Physics from MIT, and I said, "I bet you'd love to drive me around. You're Italian, and you love to drive." From day one, this has changed my life. From that one example, I started to think about my life differently.

When we started our company, there were about 12 people on the team. We're at 100 people at the moment. It's an engineering firm, and when I go off to Coach and come back, I have lots of people who come into my office and they all want to know, "What did you learn? What did you come back with?" because they know, when I come back from one of our Coach sessions, I'm full of ideas and I'm full of enthusiasm. Even the people who aren't my direct reports, who aren't in my circle that I work with every day, everybody in the company knows we're going and they want to know what we're bringing back. They see how much it touches the company and how much it changes us when we come back.

One of the tools I brought back from Coach that has affected me the most is one called The Bigger Future™. That exercise is about setting really, really big goals—thinking long-term, thinking about the things you really want to do with your life. That's the tool I've really hit some home runs with, not just in my life, but in seeing employees and friends when they got stuck, I was able to walk them through that exercise. It's amazing when somebody comes back to you a week later, a month later, and says, "Thank you for doing that exercise with me. It's really changed my life."

I know it makes me feel really good that I've been able to help them. Here's Dan who's created these tools, and they're touching people that are three, four, or five people away from him. They're reaping benefits of these things that he's brought to life, and yet they've never met him.

One of the other things I've taken away from Coach is I think the way most of us have been taught to set goals is almost backwards. People talk about setting 90-day goals, one-year goals, five-year goals, or ten-year goals. Dan takes a much bigger approach to goal setting. The way the Bigger Future sets things up is, it makes you look 20 years in the future and kind of not look at where you are now, as a starting point, but just paint the picture of where you want to be in 20 years.

Everybody's at a starting point, and you can get anywhere you want to go. There are no barriers here or limitations. You need to know where you want to go. You start with a 20-year goal and then say if that's where I'm going to be in 20 years, where would I be in ten years? Being able to open someone's mind to the idea that they don't have to just take small steps to move up to something, that they can paint the biggest picture they can imagine, then figure out the steps to get there after, it really opens their mind to a lot more possibilities than they would have come up with if they were going the other way and just trying to set a 90-day goal and the like.

What happens is you talk yourself out of it, you scare yourself away from the dream. If you just say, "Where do I want to be? What does my idea look like?" you can paint that picture. Then you start recognizing the opportunities on how to get there after you've painted the picture.

What you realize from being in Coach is, it's not just the business aspect of it. It's about your entire life. Everything, for an entrepreneur, is kind of interwoven. It's had a ripple effect on our whole life. If I'm going to have all this new free time that I didn't have before, I need some new hobbies. I started riding horses, I started computing, and then I realized I needed to be in better shape, so I started getting super healthy. Same thing with my husband, in fact.

Between us, we've lost over 100 pounds, and we've become much more athletic. We're taking care of ourselves, not just in the business but at home as well. The Coach mindset permeates how we spend our free time. It's kind of pervasive for the rest of our lives.

My biggest thing I'd like to say to Dan is, "Happy birthday and thank you." My second message is, "Keep going." I don't know what I would do if I couldn't do this every quarter and come back with newfound enthusiasm. Being in a room with Dan is like getting refueled for all the things I want to do in life. Dan has provided the inspiration, and he's given me the tools and the confidence to build whatever future I want.

*"**D**an made my impossible dream very ordinarily achievable."*

Steven Palter, M.D.
-Gold Coast IVF

For many years, I was outwardly very successful in my profession as a physician; however, there were things I struggled with, such as how to deal with the growth I was having in my business, and the long-term goals of some of the big things I wanted to achieve. I was getting increasingly overwhelmed and feeling like I didn't know how to get to where I wanted to be.

One hour after meeting and speaking with Dan Sullivan, I had a clarity of understanding of everything that was frustrating me. He provided a new model to look at life, to get to my ideal future. What I realized in that one hour was that all the advice that my mentor had given me for the past 10 years was all really Dan Sullivan thinking tools.

I was working at Yale University School of Medicine as their chief of the fertility division, and I was lecturing around the world, and teaching and doing research, but I had a dream of something bigger—something where I would have my own clinical and research center where we would do all of the leading cutting-edge work in the world.

I wanted it to be a special kind of environment where we took care of patients in a way that was unequal to anywhere else. I had this vision of creating a world-class center, and I was coming from this big bureaucratic organization where you're supposed to just stay in the system. Everyone I turned to told me it was impossible to go out and make my dream a reality.

Coach and Dan gave me both the clarity on what I wanted to do and the confidence to do it. The relationships between Dan and the other people in the Program made my impossible dream very ordinarily achievable.

Instead of incrementally growing a practice and creating this impossible thing along a linear track, Dan expands your vision of what you can do. And for that, I am eternally grateful.

One of the tools that helped me most is that every Coach meeting begins and ends with a Positive Focus®, where you talk about what went right and what was the success. It shifts your mind into what has worked instead of focusing on what has failed you, and by doing this it transforms how you do everything.

And the tools we learn from Dan are just as valuable for teaching the kids how to navigate the complexity of modern life.

Through the Coach concepts, our kids can feel self worth and avoid self criticism, which is pretty rare these days. They are also becoming very forward-looking and work on how they can realize what their goals are and how not to get beaten down by the world. They respond to this as avidly, if not more so, than any adult. The same tools that have transformed our business world are enormously important in our family life, and we've heard that from many other people in the Program—that these tools have become the core of their family relationships as well.

Having balance with your family and your personal life is an enormously important concept. You learn more than just how to have free time, how to take a day off, which frankly, many of us have never done before we were in Coach. It was always, "Work twice as hard. Stay late and finish the project." In Coach, we learn to take time off, but these are tools family members and friends can use for these issues as well.

Tools like The Lifetime Extender® and the Unique Ability process give enormous clarity to everyone who uses them.

The Positive Focus exercise where you list three wins for the day, why those wins were important, and what you could do the next day that would be a win—it really shifts you. Everyone comes home from school and work thinking about where they didn't live up to their expectations. This shifts the focus to the positive from the negative.

The Lifetime Extender tool is a mental way of trying to focus on where you want to be in the future. And for people who are feeling lost or nearing retirement or losing their job, it's a way for them to imagine a new greater or better future no matter how old they are.

Both The Positive Focus and The Lifetime Extender get you into a forward focus instead of looking backwards to where you fell short or what you've lost or what's ending. You turn around and face a bigger future that's better. This puts you right on this forward-looking focus, which enables you to let the past go and focus on all the good things that are ahead of you.

Dan calculated a way to live to be 149 years young. I want to personally say thank you for the wisdom, the guidance, and, most importantly, the friendship that has been such a beautiful part of our business and our personal lives. Thank you, Dan.

*"**D**an is an applied philosopher who helps you improve your world using the power of your mind."*

Michele Palter

Dan Sullivan is an applied philosopher because he takes the anthropic philosophical principle about how the world is and helps you to come up with principles and tools for improving your world using the power of your mind.

When you realize your world is constructed of the ideas you have about the world, then it's like an unfair advantage over the world because you kind of see what goes on. It's like "the matrix" when you see the code behind everything. You see the principles and the ideas that underguard your world if you can take a step back and see it's really your ideas that create your world.

If you get better at your ideas, or you get more strategic about how you think about your world, it's like the matrix. You kind of bend time—you can do things you didn't think you could do because you have this tool to help you step back from your circumstances to see how your thinking is affecting those circumstances.

Dan and I have collaborated on writing-related projects over the years, which has been really fun because Dan is a truly original and incisive writing voice. Reading his writing has been such a pleasure, and learning about how he communicates so effectively with all the people he interacts with has really changed the way I write fiction and also given me a way to think about my writing altogether. My writing has improved greatly working with this principle, and even though it's not necessarily what they're designed to do, one of the things that's so great about the different Coach tools is that they're so versatile.

What Dan teaches you to do at so many levels is to really think about who you're talking with, whether it's in business, on paper, or your reading audience.

The work Steve and I have done through Strategic Coach has really affected our home life as well. The kids are able to see how they each have their own strength, and they're not the same. They're starting to see and understand the things they are uniquely good at and like. Even at such young ages, they realize they don't have to have the same aims and like the same subjects. We talk about what they think their special gifts are or what they bring that's different than other people. Our oldest son will say, "Well, I tend to look at things differently than other people, and I see things that other people might miss." Pretty profound for a thirteen year old!

I want to say happy birthday Dan, from Steven, from me, and from Josh, Gabe, and Sam! They enjoy yours and Babs's company also, and it's been such a real inspiration and privilege to spend time with you and Babs and just enjoy your company. We just love spending time with you and enjoying life, really seeing what the world could be, and just enjoying the world as it is.

*"**Y**ou can have all the success in the world, but if you don't have gratitude, you're not going to be happy. "*

Joe Polish
-Piranha Marketing

My biggest impact from my introduction to Dan Sullivan and Strategic Coach has been nothing short of monumental in terms of my thinking, in terms of my growth, in terms of my relationships, and in terms of my focus. When I first heard about Strategic Coach, it was like the Apple or the Four Seasons of information products. They referred to what they produce as "Knowledge Products," and I even loved the distinction because a lot of great information isn't packaged or organized in great ways and, therefore, loses the power and the impact.

Dan has designed and uniquely packaged what they offer at Strategic Coach in a way that makes it very accessible and very usable and very personable. A lot of trainings are, "Here's the way you should live in someone else's value system." What's great about Strategic Coach is that they give you answers to many of life's challenges and business challenges and solutions on how to reach opportunities that are important to you and to entrepreneurs. However, they do it in the form of powerful thinking tools and thinking exercises. It's never about Dan or someone telling you the way to live your life. It's really about showing you a structure for how to make it work for you, with an emphasis on having not only a great business, but a great life.

One of the things I discovered through my involvement in Strategic Coach starting in late 1996 when I first heard about them was the whole notion of living in your Unique Ability. Dan's goal is to help as many human beings as possible to become aware of what their Unique Ability is, which is a talent, a skill, a behavior, an MO, that you're not only excellent at, but gives you constant, never ending energy and improvement. The power of living in Unique Ability is that it reduces suffering.

There are a lot of the driven, successful, impactful, valuable entrepreneurs on the planet, and many of these people live incredibly destructive and painful lives in spite of their financial success, fame, and impact because they pay a price for that success. It reminds me of a quote I heard that goes something like:

"If I would have known being successful was this much work, I would have stuck with being a loser."

The funny thing with Strategic Coach is they not only teach you how to be successful, but how to not sacrifice your life and everything in the process.

One of the first things I heard when I went to Strategic Coach is if you're not willing to take Free Days and give yourself the ability to rejuvenate, you're not going to get a lot out of this Program. It's not for people who want to live their lives as workaholics and justify that as what it takes to be successful. It's the complete opposite of everything I had heard from so many other trainings and this whole work ethic. That's not to say you don't work hard. It just means it doesn't become a religion that you spend the rest of your life worshiping at the altar of, "You have to sacrifice everything in order to be successful." That really impacted me a lot.

The other huge piece I learned from Coach was that money earned is a byproduct of value creation. I already operated that way, but to see a company where everything they represent was about servicing their clients and creating value and not doing anything for anyone that would not be a multiplier for them was huge for me. What I came away with—and here I am today understanding something that I learned early on—was that the two most important things to protect in life as an entrepreneur are your confidence and your gratitude. You can have all the success in the world, but if you don't have gratitude, you're not going to be happy. You don't do anything really well consistently when you're not operating at a high level of confidence.

My favorite words of what Strategic Coach has given me—the ripple effect that this has given me and thousands of other people who are successful entrepreneurs and who Dan calls Industry Transformers—are direction, confidence, clarity, and capabilities. When you follow the process Dan has created in Strategic Coach, you will definitely have more clarity, more confidence, more capabilities, gratitude, you name it. In fact, this has allowed me to develop "The Genius Network," which is my group of people who are geniuses and have enormous power, and it fits so well into what Dan does at Strategic Coach.

Dan and I have created 10x Talk, a podcast we record together where we share messages with successful entrepreneurs. The ripple effect of Dan and Strategic Coach will literally go on for centuries. As long as the planet exists, there are going to be great entrepreneurs who have been trained and have been coached and have been led to live in their Unique Ability to transform their own businesses, their own industries, their own lives. There are so many strategic byproducts that have come out of Strategic Coach and the people who participate in Strategic Coach. It is truly the one place where people can develop an E.L.F. business, which is "easy, lucrative, and fun" because most people run H.A.L.F. businesses, which are "hard, annoying, lame, and frustrating" or sometimes "hard, annoying, lucrative, and frustrating."

When you say things can be easy, most people don't believe it, and in most cases, it's not true. If you set things up properly, you truly can have an E.L.F. business, and the beauty of Strategic Coach is that they actually teach you how to set it up. They're unique in that they really want entrepreneurs to live in their Unique Abilities. What better way to spend your life—not only being excellent, but being excellent in something that gives you continual energy and growth and impacts the world in such powerful ways? I hope everyone gets tremendous value on hearing about the ripple effect of Dan Sullivan and his amazing company, Strategic Coach.

Dan, I just wanted to say it's been the trip of a lifetime, and I hope our trip lasts many dozens of more years. The impact you've had on my life and my clients' lives cannot be measured. Keep forging on. The world needs you.

*"**E**nvision who you have to be in the future when your business is ten times larger."*

Joseph Cohen
-Hoyle Cohen

The biggest single breakthrough for my business from my many years with Strategic Coach has to be the 10x Mind Expander® concept Dan teaches. When I first did the exercise, it was great. But then I did it a second time. And then a third time, and eventually it hit home for me. This was the point of inflection in my business where I realized I couldn't continue to grow unless I took a big leap forward. Dan was able to get me to finally see what I needed to do to really expand our business.

As a result of Dan Sullivan's 10x Multiplier, we were trying to grow from $1 million in sales to $10 million, which is no easy feat. And now I'm happy to report we are approaching the $8 million in revenue mark and it all happened because of that one exercise where Dan asked us to "envision where you have to be in the future when your business is ten times larger."

Being in a coaching environment is a wonderful thing, as you learn from your mentor and, without even being fully aware of it, you begin to mentor other people from what you've learned. And pretty soon, it becomes conscious and you realize that you too are changing lives. Dan doesn't fully realize the full effect he's had on my team (or maybe he does!). I'm mentoring a number of younger advisers in our firm, and I use Strategic Coach concepts with them all the time and they're loving it. Some of them don't qualify for the Coach Program yet, but as soon as they do, they are going to attend.

And just as importantly, on a family basis, about a year and a half ago, I sent my daughter-in-law to the Coach Program. She's running the family business (hotel) and in 18 short months, I've seen a huge transformation in her. When you talk about the ripple effect from being in Dan's group, being able to pay it forward with the people you love and care about, it's just so powerful.

I've also found the same breakthrough extends to other parts of my life beyond work. At this stage of life (I'm sixty-five now), I've taken the 10x Multiplier concept and applied it to my physical well-being and I'm asking myself, how do I get 10x better in terms of my health? My physical ability is the foundation for everything else in life, so I really must work at staying healthy the rest of the way.

Dan Sullivan has personally inspired me to a lifetime of learning in all realms: A life of learning in terms of business, a lifetime of learning in terms of physical well-being, and a lifetime of learning in terms of relationships. Being in Strategic Coach has been a wonderful journey for the past 15 years, and I hope to accompany Dan on the next 25 years.

"You know you've found your Unique Ability when you can do it all day long and at the end of the day you're not tired in the least."

Steven Jackson
-Attorney & Cousellor at Law

I think a man's legacy is based on the impact he has on other's lives. The American Indians say if someone is still telling your story after you're gone, you're never really gone. Dan Sullivan's story will be told for decades and decades and decades to come. I think the impact he's had on his clients professionally and personally has been very tremendous.

Before I found Strategic Coach, when I would take my one week's vacation for the year, I would come back with sand in my files. Last year, I took ten weeks' vacation with no files, no email, no phone. Thanks to Dan's teachings, I've learned how to relax and get restored so when I come back from vacation I can get back into my giftedness.

One of the main things they talk about at Coach is staying within your God-given Unique Ability. The more you're in that place, if you can seize that and stay in that, the happier you'll be, the more successful you'll be, the more impact you'll have.

Your Unique Ability is something you do extremely well that others can't or don't necessarily do. In fact, you know you've found your Unique Ability when you can do it all day long and at the end of the day you're not tired in the least and you have the feeling of a job well done.

To give you an example of how this relates to my business, I moved from trial work into estate planning. Why? Estate planning is about getting people to open up and building relationships. When you do this right and it's your Unique Ability, which it is for me, your clients will tell you where the holes are in the wall so to speak. They tell you where their difficulties are in life and then you can help solve them. I've built my business around solving my clients' problems, which correlates beautifully with my Unique Ability in getting people to open up.

To take this one step further, I like putting the pieces of a puzzle together. From a legal standpoint, I like putting the pieces together to solve my clients' issues. It's a much better fit for me than trial work. Now, I spend my time focused on staying in my Unique Ability and delegating out the parts I don't like or aren't my Unique Ability to team members.

I find when I stick with my Unique Ability, it makes me more gracious and present in relationships with those I love. I believe everything happens for a reason, and I'm thankful for a fuller life both professionally and personally because of Strategic Coach. Thank you, Dan Sullivan, for being such an influential part of my journey. I look forward to where things lead next.

*"**P**erfection, not progress, is what holds a lot of entrepreneurs back."*

Peter Kaplan
-Financial Productivity Group

I've been following Dan Sullivan for I'd hate to tell you how many years now, but three years ago, I decided to pull the trigger and head off to Chicago and embark in Coach, and it's been an unbelievable experience for me both personally and professionally. There are so many different things that have impacted my life, from The R-Factor Question® to The Strategy Circle to The Impact Filter, and working with our Ideal Clients. Absolutely everything has been just what I needed to hear.

Dan speaks about his concept of progress, not perfection, and what holds a lot of people back in their business and in life is they want to perfect something before they get going on it. Dan says it's okay just to get going and make progress along the way. For me, this was a huge breakthrough as I'm a bit of a perfectionist and would never get my projects completed because of it. Just to hear Dan share with us that you can get that 80% done really quickly and then spend the next bit of time focusing on the 80% of the remaining 20% was really powerful. After two goes around doing this, you're at 96%, as opposed to a lot of people who get paralyzed in trying to perfect things from the get-go. They don't start anything, because they want to get it right first, but often your 80% is 100% better than what other people are doing. This, for me, has been an unbelievable concept, because as I said, I am a perfectionist and in a way it's held me back.

Because I work in the financial services sector and so many of Dan's other clients are also in the financial services sector, we now speak a common language and have a common bond through Coach and assisting each other to grow and evolve, which is another huge benefit of being in Coach.

The trips to Chicago for the Strategic Coach meetings have been amazing, and I've made great friends through the Program and for my business and my family life and my health. In fact, one of the accomplishments I've had from Coach is I've lost 78 pounds.

Dan, allow me to personally wish you a happy birthday! Thank you for all your insights and thoughts these last few years together. Everyone in the Strategic Coach Program and people who've heard you speak who haven't even embarked on the Program have been touched by you. Please god, you should have another 70 years.

*"**D**an showed me how to work smarter in my business, but more than anything how to work on my business and have a personal life as well."*

Patrick Keating
-Keating & Associates Inc.

I met Dan 20 years ago at a meeting in the Dallas, Texas, area and knew right then he was the person who could help me. At the time, I was spending loads of hours each day and working too much and was frustrated. I had three young children and knew I wanted to make a change in the way I was running my business but didn't. Over the last 20 years, Dan has allowed me to learn how really to work in my business, but more than anything to work *on* my business and have a personal life as well. And over that time, we've been very fortunate as our organization has grown dramatically.

In fact, my assistant joined the Strategic Coach program for assistants when they first started it. She's still in that program 17 years later—that's how good it is. We have several other people that have joined from our firm as well. Two of my own children have entered the business, and I feel they entered the financial services industry because they saw how I had balanced my personal life and business life using the concept of Free Days™, Focus Days™, and Buffer Days™ that Dan teaches us. That's been the greatest thing for me and our team, and it's been great for my relationship with my wife as well.

Dan's concept of Free Days is 24-hour days, from midnight to midnight, where you do nothing toward making a living. You don't check emails, you don't call the office, you don't do anything work-related. I now have many Free Days. Focus Days are where you do the key things to make a living. Buffer Days become your cleanup days. Because of Dan's help, we've been able to build our entire organization around those concepts and so all of our staff understands them. We teach the concept throughout the company, so everyone knows a Free Day is free, which means we respect staff as well. We don't call them at home. We don't call them on weekends. They need to relax as much as we do.

When I'm off, my staff runs the company and I'm not involved in it. Once you start to practice the concept of Focus Days, you really see that you have to spend your day doing the thing that's most important to do to make a living and not being interrupted by all the little things we are so distracted with nowadays. Ultimately, I try to build my career now around pretty much predominantly all Free Days or all Focus Days with minimal Buffer Days in between and letting other people do all of those kinds of things because they are better at it than I am anyway.

Personally, I'd like to tell Dan thank you for sharing all the things you have learned over the years with us. I know you use your clients to push you and help you learn, but being in your Program has been a phenomenal thing for me and my family. It's meant a great deal for my associates and a tremendous thing for my clients, as I've been able to offer more value to them to help them understand the concept of not working all the time. Life is meant to be enjoyed, and

I appreciate all the things you have done for me and my family. Instilling the value that you never have to quit doing what you love doing because you reach a certain age has allowed me to have a career that's going to continue to last for many years. Happy birthday, Dan. Here's to many, many more.

*"**D**an showed me it's not about me being significant, but what significant impact I was going to have on the world."*

Roch Tranel
- The Tranel Financial Group

I started with Strategic Coach 15 years ago as a budding entrepreneur, starting in my business, wanting to have significance for my business, wanting to have significance for myself to increase the money I made for the business and for myself, personally.

I think the real value that Dan has helped me see for myself as I progress in business is that I realized it's not about me being significant, it's not about the business being significant, but it's rather about what significant impact I was going to have on the world. I know for a fact I would not have had that "Aha" or that insight without going through the Strategic Coach Program. I'm excited today to share with everybody that Dan's had a transformation on my thinking about what my purpose is in the world and how I share that purpose or have impact on the rest of the world.

I think the tools Dan shares help you think about what you're thinking about and what you should be thinking about, and bring up our time as a business owner to really think about the impact. I think one of the great tools he shared with us that helped guide me was The Lifetime Extender, which is a unique tool to help you think about the last part of your life. This tool really changed how I thought about that.

It's so beneficial to have a place to go to every 90 days to really think about how to have a bigger future and how you're really going to impact people, and to hang around other people who are having an impact so you can learn from others who are little farther down the path than you are and give you great "Aha's" and insights about what you can do.

The Coach Program just allows you to hang around people where you have permission to think about and dream about impacting the world, whereas if you did that in a group of other people, it wouldn't be seen as normal. You would be maybe put down for thinking that way or just thought of in a different way. Not in the positive light that it's intended. Strategic Coach has allowed me to surround myself with a group of people who really encourage me and foster me in my thinking.

Dan, you've really helped me with my journey, not only as a businessperson, but by helping me become an excellent role model for my children. Really being present with my wife and being a supportive, strong husband and being an excellent leader in the community and in my company to really impact as many people as possible.

The great part about being Dan's friend and being involved in his Program is that his ability to stretch my thinking has really helped me reach my true potential to have the impact I think I'm supposed to have on the world. I'm just grateful to be connected with Dan Sullivan, to call Dan my friend, and have hundreds and hundreds and maybe thousands of people be impacted based on my new way of thinking. I'm just grateful to you, Dan, for sharing your insights in a way that I can absorb them and then pass the knowledge along to others. Have a great 70th birthday, Dan. Looking forward to many more.

"With Dan's help, we've increased our asset base by over 800% and we've taken our equity 10x."

Braden Hodye
-Hodye Group

I'm the president of the Hodye Group, which is a family-owned business going on 30-plus years. I'm a third generation, and I'm in my late twenties. I joined Strategic Coach approximately eight years ago on the recommendation of business partners who were currently in the Coach Program. Strategic Coach came highly recommended to us by others in the Program on how well it worked with business processes, practices, and tools to continue to move forward.

Since I have entrepreneurship running through my blood as does the rest of our family, we were at a point in our business objective where we were getting ready to ramp up into a very aggressive growth mode. We were looking at diversifying into a number of different industries and businesses, getting into new projects and new territory that we had never researched or explored before. It was a great time for us to start at Coach. Some of our biggest breakthroughs, right from day one, came from some of the very valuable tools Strategic Coach offers that helped open up our minds and our thinking.

Once we got into some of the business processes and tools—The Bigger Future, The Front Stage/Back Stage Audit, The 10x Mind Expander, The Strategy Circle—we continued to use a lot of those tools and implement them within our businesses on a regular basis, which helped us track, delegate, hire team members, and grow our business.

Over the course of the past eight years and with Dan's help, we've increased our asset base by over 800% and we've taken our equity 10x. At the time we were starting to strategize and plan those types of lofty objectives, we couldn't see our way clear of that far down the road. How were we going to reach these objectives? What's our strategy? Strategic Coach really helped us emphasize those strategies as best as we possibly could.

Furthermore, to meet up with a group of like-minded individuals at Coach every three months has been a huge benefit. Three years ago, I started the You x 10® Program and have been in Dan's presence for all of those sessions. He's been our head coach. His knowledge and his ability to see challenges, to see where some frustrations are building from a business on an entrepreneurship end, whether it be just a business process, time management, a delegation, or figuring out how to grow 10x, he truly has a gift of seeing his way clear of those challenges and creating strategies and processes to help us entrepreneurs overcome them. Whether it's getting out of "The Gap," The Frustration Breakthrough™, or setting very lofty objectives, both for business and personal, it's been a huge benefit over all these years.

We truly are grateful for being introduced to Coach, for having the opportunity to network with like-minded individuals, to see how a first-class operation like Strategic Coach is being run, to be networked and have access to all of the team members at Strategic Coach when we need some assistance between our sessions throughout our quarters as well as having the opportunity to work directly with Dan and Babs. They truly have a gift, and they're sharing it with the business world, and we appreciate being a part of it.

There are two tools that coincide with each other that have really hit for me as a young entrepreneur working within the family dynamics of family business, growing the business substantially. One was the 10x concept—looking out and setting goals for 10x where you currently are today. That one has been the biggest one, and what has allowed me to navigate through those goals and reach my objectives is The Impact Filter. That is by far the easiest and most useful tool I employ on a daily basis that allows me to set my objectives, whether I'm going into a meeting, starting a major project, or convincing somebody of something. It can be used in so many different areas for so many different purposes that it really allows me to stay focused and continue to work toward those goals and objectives, to hit the 10x.

I would personally like to tell Dan that he has a gift and a vision, and he needs to take a lot of pride in the way he's developed that vision into sharing it with other people. Thank you, Dan, for sharing your gifts with us so we can turn around and do the same for our clients.

*"**D**an's Lifetime Extender exercise has shifted my thinking, so rather than thinking about retiring and hanging it up, I have a vision of another 50 years of contribution."*

Mrya Salzer
-The Wealth Conservancy, Inc.

It's been close to 20 years since I joined Strategic Coach, and Dan Sullivan is my hero. When I first started out, my girls were in their teens and Dan was the first person who gave me permission to delegate things I thought supermoms were supposed to do in addition to running my company—things like the grocery shopping or the cooking or doing all the laundry and cleaning. Here I was, still doing all those silly things. Delegations enabled me to free up my life so I could focus on that which is most important, which is helping change the lives of my clients and spending time with my family in a quality way. This was a huge game changer for me.

I would say there are few people who have made a bigger difference in my life than Dan. The difference has been as much by the example he sets as by what I actually learn in his classes. I live in Boulder, Colorado. It's very liberal and "republic," if you know what I mean. So to be able to get my quarterly shot of permission to be successful and to have goals and want to win has been a wonderful experience. I've always been surrounded by professionals (my husband, daughters, and parents). No one else in my family is an entrepreneur, and so watching how Dan and Babs have grown over the years and have implemented their own vision and used their own tools for their business and their lives has been so important to me. They practice what they preach, they walk their talk, and they lead from behind. The tools are great, and seeing by example how the tools are implemented makes them real and applicable.

If I had to say which tool I go back to day in and day out, the one I preach to everybody at TWC, the one I really try to live by, it's the four Referability Habits™. Specifically—Do what you say, finish what you start, show up on time, and say please and thank you.

I just know every time I'm unhappy with a service of any sort it's because one of those four habits hasn't been honored. They're easy enough. So simple and elegant! That's a gift that Dan provides the world. He breaks complex things down into the simplest forms so those who don't have complex minds can grasp and retain and implement for themselves.

Speaking of tools, another tool that has changed my life is Dan's Lifetime Extender exercise, where you imagine extending your life 20 years, or 25 years further out than you thought possible. If you knew you were going live 25 years beyond conventional expectations, what would you do now that would be different, and how would you fill that time? It's a powerful question that not many people ask themselves. This tool has shifted my thinking.

There are so many people in my life who are preparing to retire. You know, they're sort of hanging it up. I'm not ready to go out to pasture, so I now have this vision of another 50 years of growing The Wealth Conservancy and contributing to others. I'm really just beginning when you look at it that way. It's a whole different way of looking at life—one that Dan's exercise made possible.

I'm well into my sixties now. Thanks to Dan, I feel turning seventy is not such a big deal; it's just another day and I hope Dan totally enjoys his day and celebrates it to the fullest. Happy birthday, Dan! You're terrific and I am so grateful you are in my life.

To Dan, I'd like to personally say a profound thank you for making yourself and your wisdom available to us and for creating a group environment where there's a safe exchange of ideas. You provide a wonderful service, and I am so appreciative. So, thank you, Dan. I look forward to seeing you every quarter for another 50 years.

*"**D**an showed me you get paid a lot more when you offer a transformation than you do when you offer a transaction."*

Ken Losch
-Advanced Green Innovations

What Dan and Babs at Strategic Coach have offered me is an incredible structure for me to stretchmark my world and a safe place to land all the time.

Because of Coach, I'm able to create these very large goals, and I have a structure in which I can lay them out and then break them down. One of the things I learned with Dan is that nothing is actionable unless it's simple. You take a very complex situation and break it into simplicity, so complexity into simplicity equals actionable, which equals success.

About a year and a half ago, I moved into the You x 10 Program, and I'll tell you, 10x has blown my mind. Probably the biggest breakthrough I've gotten from the 10x program is when Dan, 14 months ago, said to me, "You get paid a lot more when you offer a transformation than you do when you offer a transaction."

The same week, I had a gentleman who would be a multi-billion dollar client with our technology, and he asked me how much our system was, and I told him. He said, "I don't mind you getting a little chubby; I just don't want you getting fat." I realized in that moment that we offer a transaction and not a transformation. I literally went home and asked my wife and asked my relationships, and I looked at my whole world, and I literally have cleansed all transactions from my life, and that's relationships, it's personal, business, how I deal with people in every level of my world. It has to be transformational, and it's completely changed my life.

I went home to my wife and I said, "Honey, are we transactional or are we transformational?" She said, "Most often we're transformational, but every once in a while, it's good to be transactional." You have to know my wife to appreciate that completely.

Before 10x, I had exponential goals but I had a linear execution. My trajectory of execution was slightly higher than linear in a frustrating way, and now we've been able to move the trajectory of execution up to match the exponential goals. Our company has exploded in opportunity and because we learned the difference between exponential, execution, exponential relationships, and exponential business plans versus linear.

What Dan and Strategic Coach have allowed me to do is create a structure to live a very powerful, commitment-based life and know the noise is always going to be there but that I have a structure to live in commitments and chuckle and laugh at the noise.

I really want to thank Dan and all the people at Strategic Coach for creating the structure and support that gives Dan and Babs the freedom and the opportunity to create these incredible structures, and as you're building your 10x world within Strategic Coach, that we can be just those couple of tracks behind you on the train as you're laying those out for us. So thank you so much for making a difference for many, many people around me—my family, our team members at our companies—and we're so proud to be a part of, and growing these opportunities with, everybody at Strategic Coach.

Dan, I'm honored to be your friend, to be your client, and to have crossed paths with you in this lifetime, and I thank you and Babs and your whole team for everything that you've created for all of us and, in particular, for my family and our team members. I'm so honored to be part of the Program. Thank you.

*"T*hanks to Dan, we're transforming the industry and having a lot of fun doing it."

Bob Muller
-The Leo Muller Group

A bit over three years ago, the focus of Jeep in Australia changed from what it was to something different. I own a Jeep dealership in Australia. The new focus didn't really suit me; it wasn't really what I was on about. The industry as a whole is a bit too adversarial, a bit too confrontational, a bit sort of "win-lose." There was no higher reason, there was no ulterior motive except to make more money.

I enrolled myself in the Strategic Coach Program out of Santa Monica with Adrienne Duffy and went across and did my first session, and I enrolled in their Unique Ability® Discovery Session. I was pretty sure they were going to tell me I'm in the wrong industry and that I was never going to be satisfied as long as I'm in the car industry, since it just wasn't a fit for me.

The next day, I spent a full day in a room with Julia Waller and Maureen Sullivan from Strategic Coach, coming to grips with what I really thought I was good at versus what I was currently doing. I realized there was a big gap between the two.

I loved teaching and mentoring and guiding people, so I went through and wrote out my Unique Ability—refined it, and refined it, and refined it—and came back to Australia and immediately changed my role to being a guide—to mentor and coach of my team, starting with the senior folk and working from there. And what a transformation this has made in my business, in the people that we've got here, the level of expertise we've got, the focus, the enthusiasm, the commitment to the vision.

I went from being pretty ho-hum about my job—in fact, if I'm honest, I was hating my job—to actually loving what I do. I'm loving the progress people make and the way they react when you take the shackles off them and allow them to operate in their Unique Ability and schedule their time properly and get rid of messes and all that sort of stuff. And it's made such a huge, huge difference to our business and our focus.

Not without some conflict, of course, because we're transforming an industry and a business, and not everybody is on that train yet. Some of our stakeholders are still kind of looking at us thinking that one day we'll come back to reality and run a conventional car dealership. But that's never going to happen. Thanks to Dan, we're transforming the industry, and we're having a lot of fun doing it.

Now I come to work three days a week, and I have three Free Days. And of the three days I come to work, I have two Focus Days and one Buffer Day™. Actually, I call it a "Fruffer" day, where I work at home. I know Dan won't like it—it's mostly a Free Day, but I give myself permission to do a little bit of work if I have to in preparation for a Focus Day™. It's mostly spent sitting looking at the Pacific Ocean from my front balcony or doing free activity stuff.

Before Coach, my week was just a mish-mash of going from task to task. Free Days I was always pretty good at, but there was no real delineation between Focus and Buffer. I'd find that I'd go home lacking in energy and a sense of reward, because the days weren't ones where I'd walk out energized, going, "Wow. That was a good day. We really achieved something there." There was usually something in a day that managed to take the shine off it.

The contribution Dan is making to the world through his work with entrepreneurs, I think, is almost immeasurable. The future of the world belongs to entrepreneurs, and Dan is growing those people and mentoring those people and giving them the tools to go out into the world and make a much bigger difference. Dan's legacy will be one that might not be proclaimed in the history books, but it's one that will make an immeasurable impact.

On a personal note, the greatest gift Dan's given me was in our recent You x 10 session. Dan sensed I was harboring ill will toward a business partner. He called me aside, and he said, "Bob, you need to do an Impact Filter looking at that relationship from a position of gratitude."

I did the Impact Filter and realized the relationship I had with these particular people wasn't as bad as I thought it was. The relationship was one that could be enhanced and protected and grown.

Now I say to my guys, "Every time we sit down and have a meeting, we'll start as we usually do with a Positive Focus, but we're going to do everything and address every challenge and every opportunity from a position of gratitude." That's how we start every meeting now, which makes our world a much better place and opens up the opportunities for personal and professional fulfillment immensely.

That reshifting of my approach was just life-changing for me. Thank you, Dan, for all you do.

*"**F**rank Sinatra didn't move pianos."*

Joseph Johnson
-The Duke of Dollars

One of the great lines Dan Sullivan has quoted was, "Frank Sinatra didn't move pianos." I've used this analogy when it comes to my Focus Days to keep me on track. If something comes up that would normally sideline me, I would stop and ask myself, "Does Frank Sinatra go get the dry cleaning between songs? No, he goes into the next song. If Frank's cellphone rings, does he stop and answer it because it might be someone important? No, he stays focused and keeps singing song after song after song until he's done." Using the Frank Sinatra—rest in peace—analogy, I think about Frank all the time. Frank never stopped and did other things. He just sings the songs, and when he's done, then he goes on and does whatever Frank Sinatra does when he's not on stage singing. This has been a game changer for me because so often we get pulled back into being asked to move the piano, so we have to be diligent about saying no. I'm here to sing; you find a way to get the piano moved.

Where do you start with Dan Sullivan? There are dozens of ways he's influenced not only my life but the lives of my clients. The time management system Dan teaches has had a profound effect on my life. We've all heard of Focus Days and Buffer Days, but Strategic Coach got me to turn focus-based Buffer Days into real Buffer Days and Free Days into real Free Days, which has been life-transforming. In the past 12 months alone, I've been able to go to Europe for two weeks, which required being out of the office for 20 days. Then in January, I was able to spend two weeks in Hawaii with my family. That kind of time away from my business never happened before I met Dan. I owe it to scheduling the proper Free Days, the proper Buffer Days, and the proper Focus Days.

Another great tool Dan taught us is that every time I do anything now, if I'm trying to make a decision, I use The Impact Filter. It's such a basic tool to go through, but it gives you those high insight moments that tell you, "Okay, this is why it didn't work in the past" or "This is the benefit we're going to get from this." The Impact Filter has been tremendous, and so has The Delegation Filter™. I can't tell you how many things I was doing that I shouldn't have been doing. Things, in fact, I didn't want to do. Things I didn't do well and for whatever reason, I was still doing them because I thought I was the only one who could.

The Impact Filter is a better-designed Ben Franklin, to be honest. With the Ben Franklin system, you write the pros on one side and the cons on the other. For some people, that works very well. But The Impact Filter shows you your purpose, the importance, and the ideal outcome.

Dan, I would say first, "Happy birthday." Second, I hope your thoughts on longevity are accurate, because I'm incorporating them as my own thoughts, and I hope you'll have many years of continued success.

*"**D**an showed me thinking 10x is far better than thinking 2x, because with 2x you're not really working toward becoming a different you."*

Ninad Tipnis
-JTCPL Designs

For somebody from Mumbai, India, to decide to fly to Toronto four times a year is no small decision. I travel 22-plus hours each way to make it to one day in Coach. I typically get on the plane early Monday morning and reach back home early Friday morning for that one day at Coach, which sets my quarter in motion and gets me completely on track.

What I get, though, for the time is to spend my day in a room full of ambitious people—people who are supportive, who understand your language, who understand your concerns, and people with whom you can share your journey, because they, like you, are entrepreneurs. They understand what you're going through. You can be a partner to somebody. You can be a buddy to somebody. You can get mentored by somebody. You can mentor somebody.

What I have realized is there is more than one teacher in the room. Each participant, each classmate, is a university and mentor for himself. That is what the fun thing is about Coach. The one thing that struck me right in my first session was how simple Dan makes complex things. He just cuts the noise. He strips all the complexity off the subject, and he gives you the pure essence. He gives you the core of the subject in very easy-to-understand, simple language.

Because of this, I've realized it's very easy to schedule your day. It's very easy to map your goals.

Dan has a proven system of assimilating your goals, of aligning your quarter, of aligning your life goals as far as your entrepreneurial dream goals. The system is so easy that you can kick-start right from the first session itself. Then, it just keeps on getting better and better and better.

How did I embark on the whole Coach journey? I was listening to Dan's CD in my car. He spoke about working on your thinking. It's a concept that is Dan's gift to the world, which is 10x thinking. When he was speaking on that CD, it felt like he was speaking to me. Within hours of listening to that CD, I signed up for the Program. That is how powerfully it hit me. What made me sign up was the concept of 10x thinking. Dan said that thinking 10x is far better than thinking 2x, because with 2x you're not really working toward becoming a different you. You can reach 2x by working harder, by putting in more effort, but for getting 10x results, you need to redefine yourself. You need to become a different you. That is really what struck a chord with me.

I saw that is exactly what is being practiced at each Coach workshop, which is the concept of Thinking About Your Thinking. Every time, we think about how to think better, because the results depend on the quality of your thinking. That is what we work on every quarter at Coach.

What do you say to a genius like Dan? He's easily one of the smartest persons on the planet, and I've met quite a lot of intelligent gurus. I believe in continuously educating myself, so I've attended several world-class programs, but that is just a class of art. Besides being one of the smartest persons on the planet, Dan is also one of the kindest.

Thank you, Dan. Keep making a dent in the universe, as Steve Jobs would have said. I truly believe you are offering genius-level service at its best. I'm going to wish we celebrate your honored birthday in the Coach classroom with yet another world-changing concept that you give birth to. I pray to God I am a witness to that world-changing concept that Dan brings to the world. Thank you so much.

*"**T**ime isn't a scarce resource. It's actually an abundance resource if you use it right."*

Bob Mulhern
-Colliers International

The other day, I was actually talking to a prospect about joining Coach. I said, "Look, Coach is not a program about making you feel good about yourself or trying to get you psyched up about how good you are. What it does instead is try to help you expand your capacity by giving you the tools to do that. It's very transformational; however, it's given to you in a way where it doesn't seem intimidating—you feel like these are transformations you can make. With their help, I now have the capacity and the tools. Coach is saying dig deep inside, and use these with the talents you have, and go get it done."

One of my favorites Coach tools is called The Moving Future, where you look backwards 90 days and really look at all the things you're excited about that have happened. You look at today and identify what's strong and has momentum, and you look forward and say. "Okay, what am I excited about getting done in the next 90 days?" What this allows is a lot of energy, first of all, in the process, because you realize all the good things going on, which we don't often stop and take stock of. Then, it allows real clarity on how you want to spend your next 90 days to really make the most out of them.

When I started seven years ago, I came to Coach with what seemed to be in most people's eyes a lot of momentum. But deep inside, I realized I was bumping up against my own capacity. There were only so many things I could do in a day or a week. It seemed like I was completely tapped out. I was very happy but also very tired. I basically approached Coach looking for a new strategy. I needed some kind of transitional training. What I was experiencing was, and the whole idea of Strategic Coach is, that time isn't a scarce resource. It's actually an abundance resource if you use it right.

Coach helped me become very clear on who I was and what I was doing and why I was doing it, and then went further and asked the question, "Are there certain things you should be doing?" Which, of course, there were. By doing what I'm good at and not doing the things I'm not uniquely qualified to do, all of a sudden I had more capacity for doing the things I'm good at and also more capacity for free time. This capacity concept was a game changer for me.

In speaking of free time, I was very surprised to find out when Dan talked about The Time Breakthrough, that the most important time to schedule was not work time that I figured it would be or even the preparation for work, but it was the free time. Scheduling your free time was completely different from anything I'd heard. From that, I had renewed confidence to attempt things I never would have attempted without the encouragement of Coach and the training in Coach. It also gave me tons of energy, because, all of a sudden, I was doing things I really loved doing and I was good at doing.

When I talk about Dan's concept of The Time Breakthrough, one thing he got very clear on that really rang true to me was that the concept that there's not enough time to get everything done and that we're all running out of time in so many areas of our lives is a modern problem that's come about because of all the technological advances. The Coach approach to time management is something I agreed with. This whole idea of having to be connected 24/7 can be mind-numbing—all of this information that comes my way every day that I don't really need to look at but I somehow feel compelled to look or that I would feel left out or left behind.

Dan presented the concept that you could actually pull away from the treadmill most people are on, which actually allows you to gain confidence but also allows you to see things other people can't see because they're shuffling through so much information and facts. I've learned to work with less noise coming at me. By doing so, it allows me to organize what I'm doing based on things that are really important and not just urgent, which is what a lot of this noise is.

All of a sudden, since I'm not spending my time on those things, I have time to work on things that are more important to me. Some of those being my family—and by the way, my wife and I have nine children! We've been married 26 years. People always ask, "Is it one family?" Yes, one family, one mom, one dad. Nine kids, no twins. That alone is a wonderful but time-consuming part of my life.

Dan, thank you for really opening my eyes to how abundant life can be if you have a grateful heart and you allow the gratitude to really pull the creativity out of our hearts and into our lives. I'll be forever grateful for that, as will my family.

*"**F**or me, Coach is my insurance policy moving forward."*

Christopher Phelps
-Carolinas Dental Center

When I first started Coach about three years ago, I realized that even though I had 10x my business in the first six and a half years, I was out of balance, and although I was on my way to another 10x growth, I had given up control of my business to my partners and had lost all purpose and really hadn't realized I had let that all slip away. It was at Coach meetings that I realized why our growth in our business had stalled every year and had been going down when we had such phenomenal growth for the first six years.

I realized that I had to take back control of our business and, in fact, with Coach's help, that's what I did. I ended up selling two of my four offices and getting rid of my partners. This allowed me to refocus and replant new seeds for my growth plan, downsizing if you will and consolidating. The benefit was that last year, we had a $2 million increase in revenue from the year before. The cool thing about all this was that with two offices, I did the same revenue that we used to do with four offices before I started with Coach. I thought that was pretty cool and a pretty powerful impact. I can definitely say I would not have recognized where I was at or the direction I was heading, how bad I'd gotten off course, had I not been at a Coach workshop.

Another thing I took away was what Dan said at a charity lecture where he talked about The Self-Managing Company. That was my first time getting to hear him speak in person, and I thought it was a powerful lecture, and it really gave me good guidelines to focus on my next mission and how to get us to The Self-Managing Company. I've been able to take a lot of strides toward this end and make a lot of progress along the way to get there, and I feel in a very short amount of time, I'm going to be there, and it's opening up a whole new level of opportunities for my businesses.

A Self-Managing Company means turning your business into an actual business. Most of us think we own our own business, but we're actually just glorified employees of our business, which means if we're not there, the business doesn't run, and that makes you an employee. Dan says we need to create Self-Managing Companies, actual businesses that run and operate in our absence, that have no bearing on whether we're there or not. That's kind of what I've been striving to do with my practices—make them all independent and have good team leadership in place and structured to where, if I'm not around for some period of time, it will not affect my businesses.

I can honestly say that without Dan's help and his concepts and guidelines and these workshops, I don't know where I'd be today. For me, I look at it like I'll always be a Coach workshop attendee because it's my protection mechanism against myself. Being a long Kolbe Quick Start and kind of a short Follow Thru, I tend to get distracted from the big picture, and so coming every quarter helps me refocus my GPS on where I need to go and make sure I'm on track and set goals for the next 90 days. For me, Coach is my insurance policy moving forward.

Some of my favorite tools I love are The Strategy Circle and the Kolbe concept of how we naturally strive to do things—what our natural strengths and abilities are versus what our natural challenges are. It motivated me to the point that I actually went and became a Kolbe certified trainer because it spoke to me. This was the answer I was looking for in managing people and relationships. Jim Collins talks in his book *Good to Great* about getting the right person in the right seat on the bus. For me, Kolbe was the first time I'd actually had a language to describe why this person was a good fit for this seat on the bus versus why they were not a good fit. Being able to read through my whole team and reorganize them leadership-wise based on their Kolbe score has been huge for me.

Today, I say thank you, thank you for creating a program and a structure that forces me to ask questions I would not ask myself based on my Kolbe and my nature, and to sit myself down and give me time and free time every quarter to have clarity on or create the clarity I need to refocus for the next quarter. That's just invaluable—I can't even put words to it.

"I have learned how to think differently about growth and multiplying results."

Michael Williams
-Mosaic International, LLC

I have to admit, I am a serial entrepreneur. I see opportunities and I take them—all of them. How could I resist starting an investment advisory firm with my best friend immediately following college, having no knowledge of the financial services industry? Or the time I helped launch an ice cream company with another college friend? Then, there was the small business I started with a client to invest in other small start-ups. Did I mention the non-profit I started as well? Opportunities seemed to drop in my lap, and I felt as though I had to take every one of them.

I eventually sold the investment advisory firm to my business partner. Within a year, his revenue and profitability *skyrocketed*. I was quite down on myself thinking it must have been me holding us back. I finally got up the nerve to ask him how he was experiencing so much success, and he responded, "Two words: Strategic Coach." I was intrigued, yet skeptical. I would read success stories of people in the Coach Program who claimed to have not only multiplied their income, but also significantly reduced the amount of time they were working in the business. I had been taught by my brilliant mother, "If it seems to good to be true, it usually is." I found myself rolling my eyes when I heard my friend tell me time and time again that I had to trust him and make the investment in Strategic Coach. Ultimately, he convinced me by his actions and the results he was producing.

I remember being stressed when planning to attend Strategic Coach for the first time. I could not grasp how I would be able to be away from my team and my business for two full days. Every day was a workday for me. It took a crisis for me to get excited about work. There was constant strain between work and home. I had a continual sense of fatigue. At one point, I knew I needed help when I was on a date with my wife, and I told her I had to go to the bathroom in the middle of dinner. What she didn't know was I wanted to go to the bathroom to check my email. When I came back to the table, she gave me a look only a wife can give and knew to ask, "Is everything OK at work?" I was busted. I was constantly connected to my work, and I needed help.

At my very first Strategic Coach workshop, I decided to go "all in." I heeded their advice to completely unplug and be fully present. I even left my phone in the hotel room (a habit I still practice to this day). Not only did I learn some of the most profound tools that day, but I learned a new way of thinking about my business. Buckminster Fuller once said, "If you want to teach people a new way of thinking, don't bother trying to teach them. Instead, give them a tool, the use of which will lead to new ways of thinking." Strategic Coach has mastered the ability to do just this. I have learned how to think differently about growth, about multiplying results I'm looking to achieve. This new way of thinking has enabled me to simplify my life, build a filter I run all new opportunities through, build new habits that support a bigger future, and has been the catalyst for a happier, healthier, and far more balanced, relaxed, and enjoyable life. For this, I am eternally grateful I finally joined Strategic Coach. The best part about it is now I can go on a three-week vacation and I never have to "go to the bathroom" or endure the harsh look from my wife, as I am now completely present and enjoying each moment.

I am thankful for the wisdom and genius of Dan Sullivan and for the amazing company he and Babs have built. My life has been transformed because of Strategic Coach. Through this transformation, I feel as though my unique gifts have been found and I have been empowered to bring them to the world. Thank you, Dan, for making your contribution far bigger than your reward! You inspire us all. May your ripples continue ... *exponentially*.

This book is a compilation of stories of impact from Strategic Coach clients from around the globe as a surprise to Dan Sullivan who is turning 70 this year. We hope you will be inspired and encouraged by the stories within to increase the impact of your life by joining Strategic Coach with us.

For more information about Strategic Coach, its programs for successful entrepreneurs, or its many products for entrepreneurial thinkers, please call 416.531.7399 or 1.800.387.3206. Or visit *strategiccoach.com*.

Biography of Dan Sullivan

Dan Sullivan is founder and president of The Strategic Coach Inc. A visionary, an innovator, and a gifted conceptual thinker, Dan has over 40 years' experience as a highly regarded coach to top entrepreneurs. Dan's strong belief in and commitment to the power of the entrepreneur is evident in all areas of Strategic Coach and its successful coaching program, which works to help talented, successful, and ambitious entrepreneurs grow 10x while simplifying their lives.

He is author of over 30 publications, including *The 80% Approach*, *The Dan Sullivan Question*, *Creative Destruction*, and *How The Best Get Better®*. He is also co-author of *The Laws of Lifetime Growth*.

Dan is married to Babs Smith, his partner in business as well as in life. They jointly own and operate Strategic Coach, which has offices in Toronto, Chicago, and the UK, and new workshops starting regularly across North America and the UK. Dan and Babs reside in Toronto.